Web Development from Beginner to Paid Professional

Coding Challenges & Solutions

The smartest way to learn html and css

2nd Edition

Bolakale Aremu

Charles Johnson Jr.

Ojula Technology Innovations

Web Development from Beginner to Paid Professional
Coding Challenges and Solutions
The smartest way to learn html and css

Copyright © Ojula Technology Innovations

ISBN: 9798866017270

Published in the United States

Limit of Liability/Disclaimer of Warranty

This book contains information obtained from authentic and highly regarded sources. Reasonable efforts have been made to publish reliable data and information, but the author and publisher cannot assume responsibility for the validity of all materials or the consequences of their use. All information given in this book is based on the author's own research and does not constitute technical, financial or professional advice. The author and publisher have attempted to trace the copyright holders of all material reproduced in this publication, and apologize to copyright holders if permission to publish in this form has not been obtained. If any copyright material has not been acknowledged please write and let us know so we may rectify in any future reprint.

Table of Contents

Introduction

"You don't learn to walk by following rules. You learn by doing, and by falling over." - Richard Branson.

The sets of coding challenges in this book will help you get the hang of HTML and CSS in less time than you might expect, and the knowledge will stick. You'll catch onto concepts quickly. You'll be less bored, and might even be excited. You'll certainly be motivated. You'll feel confident instead of frustrated. You'll remember the lessons you learned in *Web Development from Beginner to Paid Professional,* long after you close the book. This book is regularly updated with the latest coding challenges and solutions.

Cognitive research shows that reading alone doesn't buy you much long-term retention. Even if you read a book a second or even a third time, things won't improve much, according to research.

Forget highlighting or underlining. Marking up a book gives us the illusion that we're engaging with the material, but studies show that it's an exercise in self-deception. It doesn't matter how much yellow you paint on the pages, or how many times you review the highlighted material. By the time you get to Chapter 50, you'll have forgotten most of what you highlighted in Chapter 1.

This all changes if you read less and do more—if you read a short passage and then immediately put it into practice. Washington University researchers say that being asked to retrieve information increases long-term retention by four hundred percent. That may seem implausible, but by the time you finish this book, I think you'll believe it.

Practice also makes learning more interesting. Trying to absorb long passages of technical material puts you to sleep and kills your motivation. Ten minutes of reading followed by twenty minutes of challenging practice keeps you awake and spurs you on, and it keeps you honest.

If you only read, it's easy to kid yourself that you're learning more than you are. But when you're challenged to produce the goods, there's a moment of truth. You know that you know—or that you don't. When you find out that you're a little shaky on this point or that, you can review the material, then re-do the exercise. That's all it takes to master a HTML and CSS book from beginning to end.

I've talked with many readers who say they thought they had a problem understanding technical concepts. But what looked like a comprehension problem was really a retention problem. If you get to Chapter 50 and everything you studied in Chapter 1 has faded from memory, how can you understand Chapter 50, which depends on your knowing Chapter 1 cold?

The read-then-practice approach embeds the concepts of each chapter in your long-term memory, so you're prepared to tackle material in later chapters that builds on top of those concepts. When you're able to remember what you read, you'll find that you learn HTML and CSS quite readily.

Before You Begin

There are at least 50 questions in each set of challenges in this book. Write your answers or solutions to each set of challenges in a clean notepad or your favorite text editor, such as Visual Studio Code. Then compare your answers with mine and score yourself. There's no time limit for these challenges. Just take your time.

If some of your answers are incorrect, it's nothing to worry about. You can always go back to them later and try again. You'll really learn when you try, try again, and sometimes the third time's the charm.

If a question is too easy for you to bother with, just skip it. Boredom is not part of the curriculum here. The answers or solutions to each set of questions are provided later in this book.

Although the solution to every challenge is provided later in this book, feel free to cross-check on your browser as well. I highly recommend using the Google Chrome browser.

Question Set 1

1. The file that creates a webpage is made up of nothing but
_______. Answer with one word.

2. When you name the file that creates a webpage, what are
the last 5 characters of the filename?

3. When you name a file that creates *styles* for a webpage,
what are the last 4 characters of the filename?

4. What type of program—Chrome, Firefox, Internet
Explorer, and Safari are examples—assembles a webpage
from HTML and CSS files? Answer with one word.

5. You can see the name of a webpage's HTML file in the
browser's _____________ (2 words).

6. If the following URL appears in the browser's address
bar, what is the name of the file that most likely created the
page? https://www.ojulaweb.com.

7. Typically, an HTML file is stored on the web host's
_________ (1 word).

8. What portion of the following URL is the file name?
https://www.ojulaweb.com/html-css/1.html.

9. In one word, what is this? <p>.

10. If <p> is the opening tag, what is the closing tag?

11. What are the two characters that begin and end all
HTML tags?

12. Code 2 paragraphs with the following markups only:

- I am the first paragraph
- I am the second paragraph
- </p>
- <p>
- <p>
- </p>

13. What is missing in this markup? (two words)
<p>This.</p><p>That.</p>.

14. Use only html tags to print the following paragraph exactly as written below. It is a description of a book. Author names and titles should be underlined, and adjectives should be italicized and bolded exactly as shown:

One particular book which is recommended reading is <u>The Street Lawyer</u> by <u>John Grisham</u>. This book is about a lawyer who begins re-evaluating his priorities in life when a bad incident occurs within his law firm. Consequently, he becomes acquainted with the inner city streets, and realizes the harsh existence of the homeless, and vows to give them a chance in the courts. <u>The Street Lawyer</u> is a ***great*** book. It is ***well written*** and ***interesting***. Other books by <u>John Grisham</u> include <u>The Firm</u>, <u>The Pelican Brief</u>, and <u>The Client</u>.

15. <h3> is a tag for a _________.

16. How many standard sizes of headings are there? Answer with a numeral.

17. What is the opening tag for the smallest heading?

18. There's one type of heading that should be only one-to-a-page. Type its opening tag.

19. What are the last 4 characters of a file that contains nothing but statements like this?

```
p {

  font-family: "Times New Roman", Times,
serif;

}
```

20. Type the first 3 characters of CSS code that specifies styling for paragraphs.

21. Type the first four characters of CSS code that specifies styling for the smallest heading.

22. Fill in the blank in this CSS code snippet.

```
_______ "Trebuchet MS", Helvetica, sans-
serif;
```

23. Use these pieces of code to style a paragraph. Tahoma is the first font in the stack.

Tahoma p : } font-family { Geneva , , sans-serif ;

24. Style the largest heading using this font stack: Arial, Helvetica, sans-serif.

25. Write all three lines of styling code for the second-largest heading that specify Verdana, Geneva, and sans-

serif as the font stack. View answer.

26. The link to the CSS file goes in which section of the HTML file? The answer is 4 characters long. View answer.

27. Use these pieces of code to form a CSS link code.

```
stylesheet = styles text / href " type .
link css " css > css " rel " / = = <   " "
"
```

28. Assuming that a CSS file is named "mystyles.css" and it is in a subdirectory named "mycss" write the CSS link code.

29. Write the complete CSS link code. Assume that the CSS file is in the same directory as the HTML file and that its name is "s1.css".

30. What are the first 10 characters of the CSS code for specifying how big you want a font size?

31. What is the CSS term for specifying whether text is bold?

32. When you specify font-weight by a number, how many font-weights are there? Answer with a numeral.

33. In CSS, when the color specification begins with #, how many more characters does it take to define the color? Answer with a numeral.

34. Use the pieces of code below to create a class of heading named "standout".

```
standout . ff0000 color h2 : # } { ;
```

35. Create a class of paragraphs named "bright" that colors text #8b008b.

36. Create a class that isn't tied to an element that specifies any color you like. Create the color specification by using any random combination of numbers 0 through 9 and a through f. Don't worry about what the actual color is. Use *conspicuous* as the class name.

37. Write a paragraph including opening and closing html tags and the text *This is how you do it,* assigning it the class "full_color".

38. Write html and CSS codes for the following simple paragraph:

This is what red color is.

Make sure you apply red color to only the word *red.* The class name is *shocking.*

39. What is the difference between DIV and SPAN in HTML?

40. What are the tags used to separate a section of texts?

41. Which are two semantic tags included in HTML5 version?

42. Use the pieces of code below to create an empty 2-row table with 2 cells in each row.

<table> </td> </td> </td> </td> <td> <td> <td> <td> </tr>

```
</tr> <tr> <tr>
```

43. Code the first line of the CSS styling that this HTML code refers to.

```
<ul class="special">
```

44. Style a numbered lists 3/4 of normal font size.

45. Style all ordered lists on a index.html page with the same margin all-around. Use 1.7em for the size of the margin.

46. Style all the items in a list so they're separated by .25 em.

47. Style both bullet and numbered lists so they're inset 2 ems on the left. Do it in 3 lines of code. Specify the inset without specifying the 0 margins.

48. To add spacing between cells, what keyword do you use?

49. Code 3 lines of CSS that add 1 em of space between cells.

50. Specify a minimal solid black border and a half em of padding for data cells.

51. For a table heading, specify no padding for the top and bottom and 1 em of padding right and left.

Question Set 2

1. In a form tag, a PHP script is only one kind of program that can be called to process data. Name another language, mentioned in the book, that might be used.

2. Code the form tag that produces this string of characters in the browser's address bar. Assume that the program srch.php has been called. Specify a method.

http://www.xyz.com/search?qt=dismax&sort=score+desc&query=loris&submit=

3. Code a form tag that specifies y.php to process the data. Use the more secure method.

4. Fill in the blank:

```
<input type=_______ name="surname" size="25"

maxlength="40">
```

5. Use the following pieces of code to create a one-line text field:

```
"city_or_town" maxlength = input "text"
size name = type "40" "25" > < = =
```

6. Fill in the blank:

```
<textarea _____="message" rows="8"
cols="30">
```

7. Use the following pieces of code to code the opening and closing tags for a textarea that is 40 columns wide.

"comment" < textarea = name = cols > rows / "40" "5" > <
=

8. Fill in the blank:

```
<input type=____ value="Submit this form">
```

9. The image file, ojula.png, is in the same directory as the HTML file. Fill in the blank so that ojula is a submit button.

```
<input  type=____  src="btn.png"
alt="Submit" width="72" height="18">
```

10. Fill in the blank to code a radio button:

```
<input ____ name="found-thru"
value="Google" checked="checked"> Google
```

11. Use the following pieces of code to code a radio button.

"industry" Software "software" "radio" value input name type > < = = =

12. In a group of checkboxes, how is each checkbox distinguished from the others? Answer with one word.

13. Code a checkbox named "car" that tells the processing program that the "VW" box has been checked. The checkbox is checked.

14. Fill in the blank.

```
<input type="radio" name="gender" id="r1"
value="female">

<label for=____>Female</label>
```

15. Use the pieces of code in the input tag to code the label.

```
<input type="text" name="lastname"
id="lastname" size="25" maxlength="40">
```

16. What is the opening tag to display text describing the form elements in the group?

17. Which of the following html tags can not be styled with CSS?

```
A. <body>
B. <div>
C. <p>
D. <h1>
E. <html>
```

18. In the following code, how many boxes do you see? Type a numeral.

```
<div>

  <h3>Here comes a greeting.</h3>

  <p>Hello World!</p>

</div>
```

19. If you want to make a div narrower than the window it's in, what keyword do you employ?

20. To explicitly specify the browser default of 100% width and 1em font-size, what element do you style?

21. When you're specifying a margin for a div, what is the keyword that centers the div?

22. Use the following pieces of code to center a div:

margin } auto { 0 auto 0 : ; div

23. Fill in the blank.

To position divs side-by-side, you must assign them widths that add up to no more than _____ of the width of the box that contains them.

24. Fill in the blank. If you want to position divs side-by-side, you must override their default block display, by using the keyword ______.

25. Use HTML tags only to create the table shown in Figure 2.1.

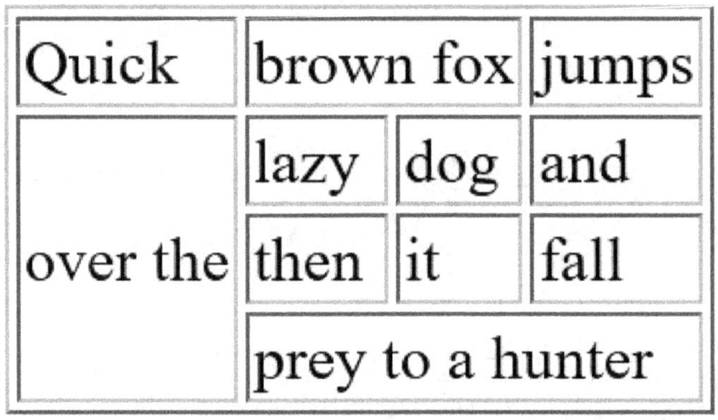

Figure 2.1: A simple HTML table

26. On your computer desktop, create a new folder and give it the name *img*. Download or take a screenshot of the image in Figure 2.2 and save it with the name *flower.jpg*. Put this image in the *img* folder. Use HTML and CSS only to display an image overlay effect shown in Figure 2.3 when you hover your mouse. Name your html file *flower.html* and your css file *styles.css*.

Figure 2.2: flower.jpg

Figure 2.3: An image overlay effect of flower.jpg

27. Use HTML only to create the simple Travel Reservation Form shown in Figure 2.4. For *Tour Packages*, use London, Germany and New York. Allow selection of more than one check box.

Travel reservation form

*** denotes mandotory**

Full name*:

FirstName LastName

Email address*:

Select Tour Package* :

London

Arrival date*:

m/d/y

Number of persons*:

What would you want to avail?*
Boarding ☐
Fooding ☐
Sight seeing ☐

Discount Coupon code:

Terms and conditions*
◉ I agree   ○ I disagree

Complete reservation

Figure 2.4: A Travel reservation form

28. Create the navigation bar shown in Figure 2.5. Name your html file *navigation_bar.html* and your css file *styles.css*.

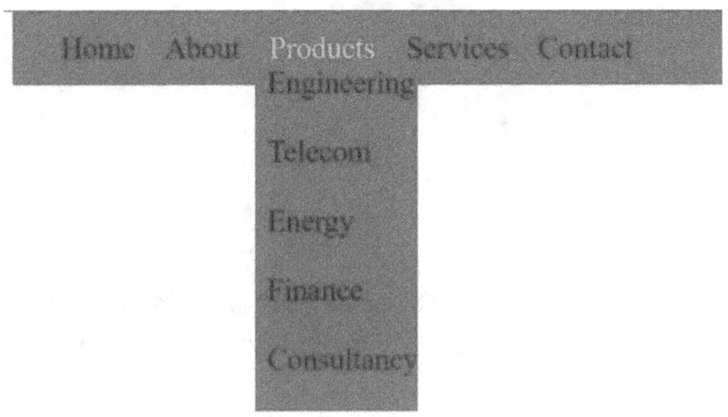

Figure 2.5: A navigation bar

29. Use HTML and CSS only to create the grid shown in Figure 2.6. There are six paragraphs in the grid. Name your html file *css_grid.html* and your css file *styles.css*. Feel free to substitute some other text for each paragraph if you wish.

Figure 2.6: A CSS Grid

30. Create the corner ribbon shown in Figure 2.7. Name your html file *corner_ribbon.html* and your css file *styles.css*. Feel free to substitute some other background color if you wish.

Figure 2.7: A css ribbon

31. Create a square of 300 pixels each side in an *index.html* file. Give your square a background color of magenta. Now, style your square in such a way that when you hover your mouse pointer on it, it changes to a circle with cyan background color after a delay of 1 second.

32. Modify your style in question 31 so that when you hover your mouse pointer on your square it changes to a circle immediately. Then after a delay of 1 second, the background color changes to cyan in a duration of 2 seconds.

33. Modify your style in question 32 so that when you hover your mouse pointer on the square the background color takes 1 second to change, and *then* the border radius takes 5 seconds to change.

34. Create 4 squares each 100 pixels in size and with a turquoise background color. Put a margin of 20 pixels on the top and bottom, and 0 pixels on the left and right of each square. Style the squares in such a way that when you hover over *any* of them, they *all* move 500 pixels straight to the right in a duration of 3 seconds.

35. Add more transition properties to the CSS you created in question 34 so that when you hover over *any* of the squares (1 to 4 from top to bottom), they all move to their destination (500 pixels to the right) in such a way that the *4th* one arrives *first*, the 2nd arrives next, while the first and second squares arrive last at the same time.

Hint: Use the *nth-of-type ( )* css property and the *cubic-bezier* transition-timing function.

36. In the <body></body> section of a new *index.html* file, create a section, a div, and an id of "RGBA". Now, in your *app.css*, style the section with a width of 500 pixels, a height of 500 pixels, and a background color of cyan. Then style the div by giving it a width of 60%, a height of 60%, and a background color of white.

37. Replace the color of your div in the CSS you created in question 36 with an RGBA color that has no transparency at all. Save and view the update on your browser. Then, give your alpha channel a value of 0.7. Now, modify your *index.html* by adding the following text inside the <div></div>:

Only the background color of my div is affected by the alpha channel. This text inside the div is not affected at all.

38. What effect will it have on the text if you add the following code snippet to the background color of your div?

```
opacity: 0.7;
```

39. In the code snippet below, fill in the blanks to position the <h1> element to always be 50px from the top, and 10px from the right, relative to the window/frame edges.

```
<style>
h1 {
  __ : __ ;
  __ : 50px;
  __ : 10px;
}
</style>
<body>
  <h1>This is a heading</h1>
  <p>This is a paragraph</p>
  <p>This is a paragraph</p>
</body>
```

40. Create a fresh *index.html* file and add the following as your body elements.

```
<body>
    <div class="parent-element">
        <div class="main-element">I am the main
element.</div>
        <div class="sibling-element">I'm the
    sibling element.</div>
    </div>
</body>
```

Now, create a new *app.css* file. Now style the two elements as follows:

Sibling Element

- Background color is Yellow
- Padding is 15 pixels
- Border: Solid line 1.5 pixels thick, with a color of `#81adc8ff`

Main Element

- Background color: Blue
- Padding: 20 pixels
- Position is fixed, 10 pixels from the left and 10 pixels from the bottom

41. In your *app.css* file in question 40, style the parent element as follows:

Parent Element

- Position: relative
- Height of 900 pixels
- Padding of 15px
- A background color of #81adc8cd

Now, modify your main element in question 40 so that as you move down the scroll bar it gets stuck at a position of 15 pixels from the top of the screen.

Fill in the blanks for question 42 to 45.

42. There are two ways to override the browser's default layout and position an element where you want it in the window. They are absolute and _______ positioning.

43. When you want to specify the exact position of an element in the window and allow it to scroll, you use _______ positioning.

44. When you want to nudge an element away from its normal position, you use ______ positioning.

45. The browser's default positioning is _______ positioning.

46. Write a simple CSS code to style the button below such that its background color changes smoothly in half a second from white to green when you hover your mouse icon on it. Use this HTML for the button.

```
<button>Hover me!</button>
```

47. Rewrite your CSS in question 46 to change your transition-timing function to `ease-out` and the duration to one second.

48. Rewrite your CSS in question 47 to change your transition-timing function to

```
transition-timing-function: cubicbezier(.59,-0.26,.33,1.42)
```

and the duration to five seconds.

49. Write the syntax that this transition shorthand corresponds to:

```
transition: all 0.5s 1s linear;
```

50. Write the longhand that the transition shorthand in question 49 corresponds to.

Question Set 3

1. Increase the size of the element with the id of ball2 to 1.5 times its original size:

```
<style>
  .ball {
    width: 40px;

    height: 40px;

    margin: 50 auto;

    position: fixed;

    background: linear-gradient(

      35deg,

      #ccffff,

      #ffcccc

    );

    border-radius: 50%;
  }
  #ball1 {
    left: 20%;
  }
  #ball2 {
    left: 65%;

    transform: scale(1.5);
  }
</style>
```

```html
<div class="ball" id= "ball1"></div>

<div class="ball" id= "ball2"></div>
```

2. Add a CSS rule for the hover state of the div and use the transform property to scale the div element to 1.1 times its original size when a user hovers over it.

```html
<style>

  div {

    width: 70%;

    height: 100px;

    margin:  50px auto;

    background: linear-gradient(

      53deg,

      #ccfffc,

      #ffcccf

    );

  }

</style>

<div></div>
```

3. Skew the element with the id of bottom by 24 degrees to the right side along the X-axis by using the transform property.

```html
<style>

  div {

    width: 70%;

    height: 100px;
```

```
    margin:  50px auto;
  }
  #top {
    background-color: red;
  }
  #bottom {
    background-color: blue;
  }
</style>
<div id="top"></div>
<div id="bottom"></div>
```

4. Skew the element with the id of **top** -10 degrees along the Y-axis by using the transform property.

```
<style>
  div {
    width: 70%;
    height: 100px;
    margin: 50px auto;
  }
  #top {
    background-color: red;
  }
  #bottom {
    background-color: blue;
    transform: skewX(24deg);
```

```
  }

</style>

<div id="top"></div>

<div id="bottom"></div>
```

5. Create an animation for the element with the id **rect,** by setting the animation-name to rainbow and the animation-duration to 4 seconds. Next, declare a @keyframes rule, and set the background-color at the beginning of the animation (0%) to blue, the middle of the animation (50%) to green, and the end of the animation (100%) to yellow.

```
<style>

  div {

    height: 40px;

    width: 70%;

    background: black;

    margin: 50px auto;

    border-radius: 5px;

  }

  #rect {

  }

</style>

<div id="rect"></div>
```

6. Use CSS @keyframes to change the background-color of the button element so it becomes #4791d0 when a user hovers over it. The @keyframes rule should only have an entry for 100%.

```
<style>
  button {
    border-radius: 5px;
    color: white;
    background-color: #0F5897;
    padding: 5px 10px 8px 10px;
  }
  button:hover {
    animation-name: background-color;
    animation-duration: 500ms;
  }
</style>
<button>Register</button>
```

7. In question 6, notice how the animation resets after 500ms has passed, causing the button to revert back to its original color. Modify your code to make the button stay highlighted.

8. In the CSS below, add a horizontal motion to the div animation. Using the left offset property, add to the @keyframes rule so rainbow starts at 0 pixels at 0%, moves to 25 pixels at 50%, and ends at -25 pixels at 100%. Don't replace the top property in the code. The animation should have both vertical and horizontal motion.

```
<style>
  div {
    height: 40px;
```

```css
    width: 70%;

    background: black;

    margin: 50px auto;

    border-radius: 5px;

    position: relative;
}
#rect {

    animation-name: rainbow;

    animation-duration: 4s;
}
@keyframes rainbow {
  0% {

    background-color: blue;

    top: 0px;
  }
  50% {

    background-color: green;

    top: 50px;
  }
  100% {

    background-color: yellow;

    top: 0px;
  }
}
```

```
</style>

<div id="rect"></div>
```

9. In this challenge, I want you to create a 3-second animation of a round element like a circle inside Visual Studio. Give the element any width, height, margin and gradient background you like. You'll change its opacity so it gradually fades as it reaches the right side of the screen. In your animation, it should move to the right by the 100% mark of the animation per the @keyframes rule. Give the element the id of **ball**. Add the opacity property set to 0.1 at 100%, so the element fades as it moves from its left to the right (choose your desired positions for left and right).

10. Use html and CSS only to re-create the diagram shown in Figure 3.10. Make your design look like it as much as possible. Use about 200 pixels for the sizes of the three shadow boxes.

Figure 3.10: Exercise 10

11. Use html and CSS only to re-create the card shown in Figure 3.11. Make your design look like it as much as possible. Use about 245 pixels for the size of the card. Also apply some border, margin, padding and shadow.

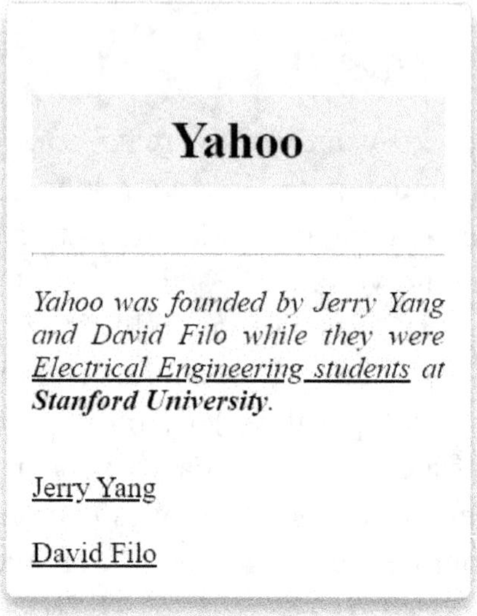

Yahoo

Yahoo was founded by Jerry Yang and David Filo while they were <u>Electrical Engineering students</u> at **Stanford University***.*

<u>Jerry Yang</u>

<u>David Filo</u>

Figure 3.11: Exercise 11

Answer Set 1

1. text

2. .html

3. .css

4. Browser

5. Address bar

6. index.html

7. server

8. 1.html

9. tag

10. </p>

11. < >

12.

```
<p>I am the first paragraph</p>

<p>I am the second paragraph</p>
```

13. Carriage return (Enter key)

14.

```
<p>One particular book which is recommended
reading is <u>The Street Lawyer</u> by
<u>John Grisham</u>. This book is about a
```

lawyer who begins re-evaluating his priorities in life when a bad incident occurs within his law firm. Consequently, he becomes acquainted with the inner city streets, and realizes the harsh existence of the homeless, and vows to give them a chance in the courts. <u>The Street Lawyer</u> is a <b><i>great</i></b> book. It is <b><i>well written</i></b> and <b><i>interesting</i></b>. Other books by <u>John Grisham</u> include <u>The Firm</u>, <u>The Pelican Brief</u>, and <u>The Client</u>.</p>

15. heading

16. 6

17. <h6>

18. <h1>

19. .css

20. p {   (Letter p, a space and the opening brace)

21. h6 {

22. font-family:

23.

```
p {

   font-family: Tahoma, Geneva, sans-serif;
```

```css
}
```

24.

```css
h1 {

font-family: Arial, Helvetica, sans-serif;

}
```

25.

```css
h2 {

  font-family: Verdana, Geneva, sans-serif;

}
```

26. head

27. `<link rel="stylesheet" type="text/css" href="css/styles.css">`

28. `<link rel="stylesheet" type="text/css" href="mycss/mystyles.css">`

29. `<link rel="stylesheet" type="text/css" href="s1.css">`

30. `font-size:`

31. `font-weight`

32. 9. The scale for font-weight ranges from 100 through 900: 100, 200, 300 and so on. 100 is the lightest weight. 400 is normal. 900 is as heavy as it gets.

33. 6.

34.

```
h2.standout {

  color: #ff0000;

}
```

35.

```
p.bright {

  color: #8b008b;

}
```

36.

```
.conspicuous {

  color: #2572ff;

}
```

37. `<p class="full_color">This is how you do it.</p>`

38.

HTML

```
<p>This is what <span
class="shocking">red</span> color is</p>
```

CSS

```
.shocking {

color: red;

}
```

39. The difference between span and div is that a span element is in-line and usually used for a small chunk of HTML inside a line, such as inside a paragraph. Whereas, a div or division element is block-line which is equivalent to having a line-break before and after it, and is used to group larger chunks of code.

40.
 tag. Usually <br> tag is used to separate the line of text. It breaks the current line and conveys the flow to the next line.

<p> tag. This contains the text in the form of a new paragraph.

<blockquote> tag. It is used to define a large quoted section. If you have a large quotation, then put the entire text within <blockquote>..........</blockquote> tag.

41. The <article> and <section> tags are two new tags that are included in HTML5. Articles can be composed of multiple sections that can have multiple articles. An article tag represents a full block of content which is a section of a bigger whole.

42.

```
<table>
  <tr>
    <td></td>
```

```
    <td></td>
  </tr>
  <tr>
    <td></td>
    <td></td>
  </tr>
</table>
```

43. `ul.special {`

44.

```
ol {

  font-size: .75em;

}
```

45.

```
ol {

  margin: 1.7em;

}
```

46.

```
li {

  margin-bottom: .25em;

}
```

47.

The correct code:

```css
ul, ol {

  margin-left: 2em;

}
```

48. border-spacing

49.

```css
table {

  border-spacing: 1em;

}
```

50.

```css
td {

  border: 1px solid black;

  padding: .5em;

}
```

51.

```css
th {

  padding: 0 1em 0 1em;

}
```

Answer Set 2

1. Any of these: Ruby, Python, Perl, Java, or C#

2. `<form action="srch.php" method="get">`

3. `<form action="y.php" method="post">`

4. "text"

5. `<input type="text" name="city_or_town" size="25" maxlength="40">`

6. name

7. `<textarea name="comment" rows="5" cols="40"></textarea>`

8. "submit"

9. "image"

10. type="radio"

11. `<input type="radio" name="industry" value="software"> Software`

12. value

13. `<input type="checkbox" name="car" value="VW" checked="checked">`

14. "rl"

15. `<label for="lastname">Last name</label>`

16. <legend>

17. E

18. 3. The div, the heading, and the paragraph.

19. width

20. body

21. auto

22.

```
div{

margin: 0 auto 0 auto;

}
```

23. 100%

24. float

25.

```
<table border="1">

<tr>

<td>Quick</td>

<td colspan="2">brown fox</td>

<td>jumps</td>

</tr>
```

```html
<tr>

<td rowspan="3">over the</td>

<td>lazy</td>

<td>dog</td>

<td>and</td>

</tr>

<tr>

<td>then</td>

<td>it</td>

<td>fall</td>

</tr>

<tr>

<td colspan="3">prey to a hunter</td>

</tr>

</table>
```

26.

HTML Code:

```html
<!DOCTYPE html>

<html lang="en">

<head>
```

```html
    <meta charset="UTF-8">

    <meta http-equiv="X-UA-Compatible"
content="IE=edge">

    <meta name="viewport" content="width=device-
width, initial-scale=1.0">

    <link rel="stylesheet" href="styles.css">

    <title>Using HTML and CSS to display an image
overlay effect on hover of the pansy flower</title>

</head>

<body>

    <figure class="hover-
img"><strong>Preview:</strong><br>

        <img src="/img/flower.jpg"/>

        <figcaption>

          <h3>Pansy <br/>Flower</h3>

        </figcaption>

    </figure>

</body>

</html>
```

CSS Code:

```css
.hover-img {

  background-color: #000;

  color: #fff;
```

```css
  display: inline-block;

  margin: 8px;

  max-width: 250px;

  min-width: 240px;

  overflow: hidden;

  position: relative;

  text-align: center;

  width: 100%;
}
.hover-img * {
  box-sizing: border-box;

  transition: all 0.45s ease;
}
.hover-img:before,
.hover-img:after {
  background-color: rgba(0, 0, 0, 0.5);

  border-top: 32px solid rgba(0, 0, 0, 0.5);

  border-bottom: 32px solid rgba(0, 0, 0, 0.5);

  position: absolute;

  top: 0;

  bottom: 0;
```

```css
    left: 0;

    right: 0;

    content: '';

    transition: all 0.3s ease;

    z-index: 1;

    opacity: 0;

    transform: scaleY(2);

}

.hover-img img {

    vertical-align: top;

    max-width: 100%;

    backface-visibility: hidden;

}

.hover-img figcaption {

    position: absolute;

    top: 0;

    bottom: 0;

    left: 0;

    right: 0;

    align-items: center;

    z-index: 1;
```

```css
    display: flex;

    flex-direction: column;

    justify-content: center;

    line-height: 1.1em;

    opacity: 0;

    z-index: 2;

    transition-delay: 0.1s;

    font-size: 24px;

    font-family: sans-serif;

    font-weight: 400;

    letter-spacing: 1px;

    text-transform: uppercase;
}
.hover-img:hover:before,
.hover-img:hover:after {
    transform: scale(1);

    opacity: 1;
}
.hover-img:hover > img {
    opacity: 0.7;
}
```

```css
.hover-img:hover figcaption {
  opacity: 1;
}
```

27.

```html
<div>
    <h1>Travel reservation form</h1>
    <h3>* denotes mandotory</h3>
    <form id="registration_form" method="POST">
        <label>Full name*:</label><br>
        <input type="text" name="full_name"
placeholder="FirstName LastName"
autofocus="autofocus" value=""><br><br>
        <label>Email address*:</label><br>
        <input type="text" name="email_addr"
value=""><br><br>
        <label>Select Tour Package* :</label><br>
          <select name="package">
            <option value="London" >London</options>
            <option value="Germany" >Germany</options>
            <option value="New York" >New York</options>
          </select><br><br>
        <label>Arrival date*:</label><br>
        <input type="text" name="arv_dt"
```

```html
placeholder="m/d/y" value=""><br><br>

            <label>Number of persons*:</label><br>

    <input type="text" name="persons"
value=""s><br><br>

        <label>What would you want to
avail?*</label> <br>

    Boarding<input type="checkbox"
name="facilities[]" value="boarding"  ><br>

    Fooding<input type="checkbox"
name="facilities[]" value="fooding"  ><br>

    Sight seeing<input type="checkbox"
name="facilities[]" value="sightseeing"  ><br><br>

     <label>Discount Coupon code:</label><br>

    <input type="text" name="dis_code"
value=""><br><br>

         <label>Terms and conditions*</label><br>

    <input type="radio" name="tnc" value="agree"
checked>I agree

    <input type="radio" name="tnc"
value="disagree" >I disagree<br><br>

    <button type="submit" class="btn btn-large
btn-primary" name="submit">Complete
reservation</button>

    </form>

    </div>
```

28.

HTML Code:

```html
<!DOCTYPE html>

<html lang="en">

<head>

    <meta charset="UTF-8">

    <meta http-equiv="X-UA-Compatible" content="IE=edge">

    <meta name="viewport" content="width=device-width, initial-scale=1.0">

    <link rel="stylesheet" href="styles.css">

    <title>A simple navigaiton bar</title>

</head>

<body>

    <nav>

        <ul>

        <li><a href="#">Home</a></li>

        <li><a href="#">About</a></li>

        <li>

        <a href="#">Products</a>

        <ul>

        <li><a href="#">Engineering</a></li>

        <li><a href="#">Telecom</a></li>
```

```html
        <li><a href="#">Energy</a></li>

        <li><a href="#">Finance</a></li>

        <li><a href="#">Consultancy</a></li>

        </ul>

        </li>

        <li><a href="#">Services</a></li>

        <li><a href="#">Contact</a></li>

        </ul>

    </nav>

</body>

</body>

</html>
```

CSS Code:

```css
nav {

    display: block;

    position: absolute;

    top: 0;

    width: 100%;

    background-color: green;

    }

    li{
```

```css
    list-style-type: none;

    display: inline;

    margin-right: 20px;

    font-size:25px

    }

    a:link {

    color: #fff;

    text-decoration: none;

    }

    a:hover {

    color: orange;

    text-decoration: none;

    }

    li > ul {

    display: none

    }

    li:hover ul {display: block; position: absolute;
left:200px;background-color:green;margin:0;}

    li:hover ul li a:link{display: block;margin-
left:-30px;}
```

29.

HTML Code:

```html
<!DOCTYPE html>

<html lang="en">

<head>

    <meta charset="UTF-8">

    <meta http-equiv="X-UA-Compatible"
content="IE=edge">

    <meta name="viewport" content="width=device-
width, initial-scale=1.0">

    <link rel="stylesheet" href="styles.css">

    <title>A CSS Grid</title>

</head>

<body>

    <div class="container">

        <div class="row">

        <div class="col1">

        <p>Lorem ipsum dolor sit amet, consectetuer
adipiscing elit, sed diam nonummy nibh euismod
tincidunt ut laoreet dolore magna aliquam erat
volutpat. Ut wisi enim ad minim veniam, quis nostrud
exerci tation ullamcorper suscipit lobortis nisl ut
aliquip ex ea commodo consequat.</p>

        </div>

        <div class="col2">

        <p>Lorem ipsum dolor sit amet, consectetuer
adipiscing elit, sed diam nonummy nibh euismod
```

tincidunt ut laoreet dolore magna aliquam erat
volutpat. Ut wisi enim ad minim veniam, quis nostrud
exerci tation ullamcorper suscipit lobortis nisl ut
aliquip ex ea commodo consequat.</p>

</div>

<div class="col3">

<p>Lorem ipsum dolor sit amet, consectetuer
adipiscing elit, sed diam nonummy nibh euismod
tincidunt ut laoreet dolore magna aliquam erat
volutpat. Ut wisi enim ad minim veniam, quis nostrud
exerci tation ullamcorper suscipit lobortis nisl ut
aliquip ex ea commodo consequat.</p>

</div>

</div>

<div class="row">

<div class="col1">

<p>Lorem ipsum dolor sit amet, consectetuer
adipiscing elit, sed diam nonummy nibh euismod
tincidunt ut laoreet dolore magna aliquam erat
volutpat. Ut wisi enim ad minim veniam, quis nostrud
exerci tation ullamcorper suscipit lobortis nisl ut
aliquip ex ea commodo consequat.</p>

</div>

<div class="col2">

<p>Lorem ipsum dolor sit amet, consectetuer
adipiscing elit, sed diam nonummy nibh euismod
tincidunt ut laoreet dolore magna aliquam erat
volutpat. Ut wisi enim ad minim veniam, quis nostrud
exerci tation ullamcorper suscipit lobortis nisl ut

```
aliquip ex ea commodo consequat.</p>

        </div>

        <div class="col3">

        <p>Lorem ipsum dolor sit amet, consectetuer
adipiscing elit, sed diam nonummy nibh euismod
tincidunt ut laoreet dolore magna aliquam erat
volutpat. Ut wisi enim ad minim veniam, quis nostrud
exerci tation ullamcorper suscipit lobortis nisl ut
aliquip ex ea commodo consequat.</p>

        </div>

        </div>

        </div>

</body>

</body>

</html>
```

CSS Code:

```css
.container, .row {

    width: 100%;

    }

    .row:before, .row:after {

        display: table;

        content: "";

    }
```

```css
.row:after {

  clear: both;

}

.col1, .col2, .col3 {

float: left;

width:25.333333333%;

margin:1%;

padding:1%;

}
```

30.

HTML Code:

```html
<!DOCTYPE html>

<html lang="en">

<head>

    <meta charset="UTF-8">

    <meta http-equiv="X-UA-Compatible" content="IE=edge">

    <meta name="viewport" content="width=device-width, initial-scale=1.0">

    <link rel="stylesheet" href="styles.css">

    <title>A Corner Ribbon</title>

</head>
```

```html
<body>

    <div class="ribbon">

        <a href="#">Best value pack</a>

    </div>

</body>

</body>

</html>
```

CSS Code:

```css
.ribbon {

    background-color: #a00;

    overflow: hidden;

    white-space: nowrap;

    /* top left corner */

    position: absolute;

    left: -50px;

    top: 40px;

    /* for 45 deg rotation */

    -webkit-transform: rotate(-45deg);

        -moz-transform: rotate(-45deg);

        -ms-transform: rotate(-45deg);

        -o-transform: rotate(-45deg);
```

```css
        transform: rotate(-45deg);

    /* for creating shadow */

    -webkit-box-shadow: 0 0 10px #888;

        -moz-box-shadow: 0 0 10px #888;

            box-shadow: 0 0 10px #888;

    }

    .ribbon a {

        border: 1px solid #faa;

        color: #fff;

        display: block;

        font: bold 100% 'Helvetica Neue', Helvetica,
Arial, sans-serif;

        margin: 1px 0;

        padding: 10px 50px;

        text-align: center;

        text-decoration: none;

        /* for creating shadow */

        text-shadow: 0 0 5px #444;

    }
```

31.

```
HTML Code:

<!DOCTYPE html>
```

```html
<html lang="en">

<head>

    <meta charset="UTF-8">

    <meta http-equiv="X-UA-Compatible"
content="IE=edge">

    <meta name="viewport" content="width=>, initial-
scale=1.0">

    <title>Transition</title>

    <link rel="stylesheet" href="styles.css">

</head>

<body>

    <h1>Transitions</h1>

    <div class="square"></div>

</body>

</html>
```

CSS Code:

```css
.square {

    width: 300px;

    height: 300px;

    background-color: magenta;

    transition: 1s;

}
```

```css
.square:hover {

    background-color: cyan;

    border-radius: 50%;

}
```

Comment: In CSS, a square of side 300 pixels changes to a circle of radius 150 pixels when a border radius of 50% is applied to it. The above code also illustrates an important CSS property called *Transition*.

32.

CSS Code:

```css
.square {

    width: 300px;

    height: 300px;

    background-color: magenta;

    transition: background-color 1s 2s;

}
.square:hover {

    background-color: cyan;

    border-radius: 50%;


}
```

33.

```css
.square {
```

```css
    width: 300px;

    height: 300px;

    background-color: magenta;

    transition: background-color 1s, border-radius
5s;

}

.square:hover {

    background-color: cyan;

    border-radius: 50%;

}
```

34.

HTML Code:

```html
<!DOCTYPE html>

<html lang="en">

<head>

    <meta charset="UTF-8">

    <meta http-equiv="X-UA-Compatible"
content="IE=edge">

    <meta name="viewport" content="width=>, initial-
scale=1.0">

    <title>Transition Timing Function</title>

    <link rel="stylesheet" href="styles.css">

</head>
```

```html
<body>

    <h1>Transitions</h1>

    <div class="square"></div>


    <section>

        <div></div>

        <div></div>

        <div></div>

        <div></div>

    </section>

</body>

</html>
```

CSS Code:

```css
/*Illustration of Transition Timing Function*/
section div {

    height: 100px;

    width: 100px;

    background-color: turquoise;

    margin: 20px 0px;

    transition: margin-left 3s;

}
```

```css
section:hover div {

    margin-left: 500px;

}
```

35. Additonal CSS Code:

```css
div:nth-of-type(1) {

    transition-timing-function: ease-in;

}

div:nth-of-type(2) {

    transition-timing-function: ease-out;

}

div:nth-of-type(3) {

    transition-timing-function: cubic-
bezier(0.7, 0, 0.84, 0);

}

div:nth-of-type(4) {

    transition-timing-function: cubic-
bezier(0.85, 0, 0.15, 1);

}
```

Comment: I didn't put the numbers in the *cubic bezier ( )* myself. I found them online at https://easings.net/. Just select the easing function you want and the appropriate values will be given. Learn more about transition-timing functions at https://developer.mozilla.org/en-US/docs/Web/CSS/transition-timing-function.

36.

HTML Code:

```html
<!DOCTYPE html>

<html lang="en">

<head>

    <meta charset="UTF-8">

    <meta http-equiv="X-UA-Compatible"
content="IE=edge">

    <meta name="viewport"
content="width=device-width, initial-
scale=1.0">

    <title>Opacity & Alpha Channel</title>

    <link rel="stylesheet" href="app.css">

</head>

<body>

    <section>

        <div id="RGBA"></div>

    </section>
```

```html
</body>

</html>
```

CSS Code:

```css
section {

    width: 500px;

    height: 500px;

    background-color: cyan;

}

#RGBA {

    width: 60%;

    height: 60%;

    background-color: white;

}
```

37.

HTML Code:

```html
<!DOCTYPE html>

<html lang="en">

<head>

    <meta charset="UTF-8">
```

```html
    <meta http-equiv="X-UA-Compatible"
content="IE=edge">

    <meta name="viewport"
content="width=device-width, initial-
scale=1.0">

    <title>Opacity & Alpha Channel</title>

    <link rel="stylesheet" href="app.css">

</head>

<body>

    <section>

        <div id="RGBA">

            Only the background color of
the div is affected by the alpha channel.
This text inside the div is not affected in
any way.

        </div>

    </section>

</body>

</html>
```

CSS Code:

```css
section {

    width: 500px;
```

```css
    height: 500px;

    background-color: cyan;

}


#RGBA {

    width: 60%;

    height: 60%;

    background-color: rgba(255, 255, 255,
0.7);

}
```

38. The opacity of the text is reduced (the text is affected).

39.

```html
<style>
h1 {
position: fixed;
top: 50px;
right: 10px;
}
</style>
<body>
```

```html
    <h1>This is a heading</h1>

    <p>This is a paragraph</p>

    <p>This is a paragraph</p>

</body>
```

40.

HTML Code:

```html
<!DOCTYPE html>

<html lang="en">

<head>

    <meta charset="UTF-8">

    <meta http-equiv="X-UA-Compatible"
content="IE=edge">

    <meta name="viewport"
content="width=device-width, initial-
scale=1.0">

    <title>Position Property</title>

    <link rel="stylesheet" href="app.css">

</head>

<body>

    <div class="parent-element">

        <div class="main-element">I'm the
```

```html
main element.</div>

  <div class="sibling-element">I'm the
sibling element.</div>

    </div>

</body>

</html>
```

CSS Code:

```css
.sibling-element {

    padding: 15px;

    background-color: yellow;

    border: 1.5px solid #81adc8ff;

}

.main-element {

    position: static;

    left: 10px;

    bottom: 10px;

    background-color: blue;

    padding: 20px;

}
```

41.

CSS Code:

```css
.sibling-element {

    padding: 15px;

    background-color: yellow;

    border: 1.5px solid #81adc8ff;

}

.main-element {

    position: sticky;

    left: 10px;

    bottom: 10px;

    top: 15px;

    background-color: blue;

    padding: 20px;

}

.parent-element {

    position: relative;

    height: 900px;

    padding: 15px;

    background-color: #81adc8cd;
```

}

42. fixed

43. absolute

44. relative

45. static

46.

button {

background: white;

transition: background 0.5s linear;

}

button:hover {

background: green;

}

47.

button {

background: white;

transition: background 1s ease-out;

}

button:hover {

```
background: green;

}
```

48.

```
button {

    background: white;

    transition: background 5s;

    transition-timing-function:
cubicbezier(.59,-0.26,.33,1.42);

    }

    button:hover {

    background: green;

    }
```

49. transition: [property] [duration] [delay] [timing-function];

50.

Each of the properties can be written in the longhand format (individually) as:

```
transition-property: all;

transition-duration: 0.5s;

transition-delay: 1s;
```

```css
transition-timing-function: linear;
```

Answer Set 3

1.

```
<style>
  .ball {
    width: 40px;
    height: 40px;
    margin: 50 auto;
    position: fixed;
    background: linear-gradient(
      35deg,
      #ccffff,
      #ffcccc
    );
    border-radius: 50%;
  }
  #ball1 {
    left: 20%;
  }
  #ball2 {
    left: 65%;
    transform: scale(1.5);
```

```
        }

</style>

<div class="ball" id= "ball1"></div>

<div class="ball" id= "ball2"></div>
```

2.

```
<style>

  div {

    width: 70%;

    height: 100px;

    margin:  50px auto;

    background: linear-gradient(

      53deg,

      #ccfffc,

      #ffcccf

    );

  }

div:hover {

  transform: scale(1.1);

}

</style>

<div></div>
```

3.

```
<style>
  div {
    width: 70%;
    height: 100px;
    margin:  50px auto;
  }
  #top {
    background-color: red;
  }
  #bottom {
    background-color: blue;
    transform: skewX(-24deg);
  }
</style>
<div id="top"></div>
<div id="bottom"></div>
```

4.

```
<style>
  div {
    width: 70%;
    height: 100px;
```

```css
    margin: 50px auto;
  }
  #top {
    background-color: red;
    transform: skewY(-10deg);

  }
  #bottom {
    background-color: blue;
    transform: skewX(24deg);
  }
```
```html
</style>
<div id="top"></div>
<div id="bottom"></div>
```

5.

```html
<style>
  div {
    height: 40px;
    width: 70%;
    background: black;
    margin: 50px auto;
    border-radius: 5px;
  }
  #rect {
```

```
    animation-name: rainbow;

    animation-duration: 4s;

  }

@keyframes rainbow {

  0% {

    background-color: blue;

  }

  50% {

    background-color: green;

  }

  100% {

    background-color: yellow;

  }

}

</style>

<div id="rect"></div>
```

6.

```
<style>

  button {

    border-radius: 5px;

    color: white;

    background-color: #0F5897;

    padding: 5px 10px 8px 10px;

  }
```

```css
button:hover {

    animation-name: background-color;

    animation-duration: 500ms;

  }

@keyframes background-color {

  100% {

    background-color: #4791d0;

  }

}

</style>

<button>Register</button>
```

7.

```css
<style>

  button {

    border-radius: 5px;

    color: white;

    background-color: #0F5897;

    padding: 5px 10px 8px 10px;

  }

  button:hover {

    animation-name: background-color;

    animation-duration: 500ms;

    animation-fill-mode: forwards;

  }
```

```
@keyframes background-color {
  100% {
    background-color: #4791d0;
  }
}
</style>
<button>Register</button>
```

8.

```
<style>
  div {
    height: 40px;
    width: 70%;
    background: black;
    margin: 50px auto;
    border-radius: 5px;
    position: relative;
  }
  #rect {
    animation-name: rainbow;
    animation-duration: 4s;
  }
  @keyframes rainbow {
    0% {
      background-color: blue;
```

```css
    top: 0px;

    left: 0px;

  }

  50% {

    background-color: green;

    top: 50px;

    left: 25px;

  }

  100% {

    background-color: yellow;

    top: 0px;

    left: -25px;

  }

}
```

```html
</style>

<div id="rect"></div>
```

9.

```html
<!DOCTYPE html>

<html lang="en">

<head>

  <meta charset="UTF-8">

  <meta http-equiv="X-UA-Compatible"
content="IE=edge">

  <meta name="viewport" content="width=device-width,
initial-scale=1.0">
```

```html
<title>Fading Ball</title>
<style>
  #ball {
    width: 70px;
    height: 70px;
    margin: 50px auto;
    position: fixed;
    left: 5%;
    border-radius: 50%;
    background: linear-gradient(
      35deg,
      #ccffff,
      #ffcccc
    );
    animation-name: fade;
    animation-duration: 3s;
  }
  @keyframes fade {
    100% {
      left: 90%;
      opacity:.1;
    }
  }
</style>
```

```html
</head>
<body>
  <div id="ball"></div>
</body>
</html>
```

10.

```css
<style>
    .box {
  width: 200px;
  height: 200px;
  background: #ccc;
  float: left;
  margin-right: 40px;
  margin-top: 10px
}

.shadow1 {
  box-shadow: 0 0 10px 0 #000;
}
.shadow2 {
  box-shadow: 0 0 0 10px #000;
}

.shadow3 {
```

```css
    box-shadow: 0 0 10px 10px #000;
}
```

```html
</style>
<div class="box shadow1"><p>Blur only</p></div>
<div class="box shadow2"><p>Spread only</p></div>
<div class="box shadow3"><p>Blur &
spread</p></div>
```

11.

```html
<style>
    h4 {
        text-align: center;
        background-color: rgba(45, 45, 45, 0.1);
        padding: 10px;
        font-size: 27px;
    }
    p {
        text-align: justify;
    }
    .links {
        text-align: left;
        color: black;
    }
    #thumbnail {
        box-shadow: 0 10px 20px rgba(0, 0, 0, 0.19), 0
6px 6px rgba(0,0,0,0.23);
```

```css
    }

    .fullCard {
      width: 245px;
      border: 1px solid #ccc;
      border-radius: 5px;
      margin: 10px 5px;
      padding: 4px;
    }
    .cardContent {
      padding: 10px;
    }
    .cardText {
      margin-bottom: 30px;
    }
```
```html
  </style>
  <div class="fullCard" id="thumbnail">
    <div class="cardContent">
      <div class="cardText">
        <h4>Yahoo</h4>
        <hr>

        <p><em>Yahoo was founded by Jerry Yang and
David Filo while they were <u>Electrical Engineering
students</u> at <strong>Stanford
University</strong>.</em></p>
```

```html
        </div>

        <div class="cardLinks">

            <a
href="https://en.wikipedia.org/wiki/Jerry_Yang_(entr
epreneur)" target="_blank" class="links">Jerry
Yang</a><br><br>

            <a
href="https://en.wikipedia.org/wiki/David_Filo"
target="_blank" class="links">David Filo</a>

        </div>

    </div>

  </div>
```